101 QUOTES FOR CHANGING THE WAY YOU THINK

BY MELISSA DE MORAL

Hello :)
My name is Melissa. Thank you for purchasing this book.
I got the inspiration to create this book, because I find myself scrolling through Pinterest & Instagram a lot, when looking for inspirational quotes whenever I feel unmotivated or lost in my (negative) thoughts.
Since I am trying to reduce the time I spend on Social Media, but still love reading through beautiful quotes that remind me of what my goal is and that inspire me to continue, I decided to create this book.
I hope it will help you as much as it helped me on our journey to a happier & successful life.
If you liked this book please leave a review on Amazon. Your kind review will help other people to find the book more easily & will encourage me to keep creating these kind of books.
Thank you!

Love, Melissa De Moral

HOW TO GET THE MOST OUT OF THIS BOOK

This book has 101 pages filled with 101
inspirational & motivating quotes.
Having a better life by just changing the way you
think, sounds too easy to be true, right?
But it is. Look up a successful person that inspires
you and sooner or later you will find out that one
of their advises is to believe that you will make it.
Have positive thoughts & visualize your dreams.
So changing your life by being aware of your
thoughts is feasible.
This book offers a daily dosis of inspiration
By reading a quote every morning you can set the
tone of the amazing day ahead of you!
The key to achieve your goals, in whatever part of
life they are, is consistency and knowing you will
make it. Always remind – **what you think, you
attract .**
When planning your day, read one quote and try
to really connect to it and to its meaning!
Enjoy this book and see it as a source of
inspiration that reminds you of why you started
your journey!

Mindset.
It's all about mindset.
From the moment
you wake up,
to the moment
you rest your
head at night.
Everything is
up to you.
Your emotions,
your thoughts,
your perceptions,
your reactions.
Every moment.

FALL IN LOVE WITH THE PROCESS OF BECOMING THE VERY BEST VERSION OF YOURSELF.

BEGIN.
Even if
you have no
idea if it
will work.

Everything is hard
before it gets easy.

Only you can turn your dreams into reality.

and you have everything you
need to make it happen

The moment you start focusing on yourself , things start falling into place.

TRUST THE PROCESS.
Know that you are exactly
where you are meant to be,
even though you may not
where you thought you
would.

Stop stressing, you're okay. You have time, slow down and calculate your steps. You got this.

REPEAT DAILY

Everything starts with m
I have the power to
change today. I take
responsibility for my life.
Great blessings are headed
my way.

No one cares for your success, so you have to care. You have to force yourself to get up early, you have to force yourself to workout.
It's your life, your dreams, your goals.

LOOK FOR SOMETHING POSITIVE IN EACH DAY

even if some days you have to look a little harder

Choose a happy life.

When you wake up each morning, take a moment and think about the kind of life you wish you'd have.
Consciously choose to have a happy life: one that is filled with love, harmony, laughter, good health & success.
Then begin your day focused on the things you can do to make this your reality.

I don't care who's doing better than me. I am doing better than I was last year.
It's me vs. me.

When you are positive in a negative situation, you win.

DEAR ME,

I KNOW YOU'RE SCARED, BUT
YOU CAN HANDLE THIS.

LOVE, ME

Old keys don't open new doors.

As long as we're breathing, it's not too late to change our story.

REPEAT DAILY

I will remain focused on my goals. Even if I have a moment of difficulty, I will not give up. I know success comes with consistency. I know that I will make it. Things will get better. No problem or challenge will stop me. Everything I deserve comes my way.

Be grateful that certain things didn't work out. Sometimes you don't even know what you're being protected from or where you're being guided to when you're in the midst of chaos. That's why you just have to trust that greater things are aligning for you.

Just because your are struggling, doesn't mean you are failing.

BE THE WOMAN YOU WOULD LOOK UP TO.

Stop worrying how it's going to happen
&
start believing it will happen.

This is just the beginning.
and it's only going to get better from here

A Queen doesn't hope
or wish.
She decides.

And just like every
other hard time, you will make
it through this one too.

The most powerful
you can do right now is to be
patient while things are
unfolding for you.

Not everyone
will understand
your journey. That's okay.
You're here to live your life,
not to make everyone
understand.

KEEP GOING.

No matter how stuck you feel. No matter how bad things are right now. No matter how many days you've spent crying. No matter how hopeless & depressed you feel. No matter how many days you've spent wishing things were different. I promise you won't feel this way forever.

KEEP GOING.

You can rise up from anything
You can completely recreate
yourself. Nothing is permanent.
You're not stuck. You have
choices. You can think new
thoughts. You can learn
something new. You can create
new habits. All that really matter
is that you decide today and
never look back.

Appreciate where you are in
your journey, even if it's not
where you want to be. Every
season serves a purpose.

To move to a new level in your life, you must break through your comfort zone and do things that are not comfortable .

Be optimistic. Think & believe that great things are coming. No matter what you are currently going through, think "there is so much to look forward to".

Two of the things you can always control in your life are your effort and your attitude.

You can.

Even if you don't believe it.
Even though it doesn't feel like
it right now.
Even in the thoughts times,

You can.

Fall in love with how hard you work, with how hard you try to be a good person, with the way you deal with problems... Value all those things that you tend to ignore about yourself and stop being so hard on yourself.

Circumstances don't define
you.
What does is how you handle
them.

Intentional days create a life on purpose.

Ask yourself if what you are
doing today is getting you
closer to where you want to be
tomorrow.

FOCUS ON THE GOOD

Today is a great day because I choose to see it as such. My thoughts are focused on the good in my life and the blessings to come.

Let go of negative feelings and thoughts. They only limit your ability to see the best in life.

Don't wait until you're
confident to show up.
Show up until you're
confident.

Create new habits. Try a new routine. Meet new people. Wake up earlier. There are too many possibilities in life to be doing the same thing.

It's the small habits. How you spend your mornings. How you talk to yourself. What you read. What you watch. Who you share your energy with. Who has access to you. That will change your life.

"If you had start doing something two weeks ago, by today you would have been two weeks better at it."

"May the next few months be a period of magnificent transformation."

If you are serious about change. You must go through uncomfortable situations. Stop trying to dodge the process. It's the only way to grow.

Successful people keep
moving.
They make mistakes but they
don't quit.

WORK HARD IN SILENCE.
BE YOUR SUCCESS BE YOUR
NOISE.

If you talk about it, it's a dream, if you envision it, it's possible, but if you schedule it, it's REAL.

Where you are
a year from now
is a reflection
of the choices
you chose to make
right now.

Every morning you have a
new opportunity to become a
happier and more successful
version of yourself.

WHEN THINGS CHANGE INSIDE
YOU,
THINGS CHANGE AROUND
YOU.

Stop waiting for friday,
for summer,
for someone to fall in love
with you.
Happiness is achieved when
you stop waiting for it and
make the most out of the
moment your are in now.

Don't give up because you had
a bad day.
Forgive yourself and do better
tomorrow.

You will never always be
motivated,
so you must learn to always be
disciplined.

MANIFEST TIP
Take the time to get crystal clear on exactly what it is that you desire to manifest. Think through as many details as possible. when you kind of know what you want, you kind of get what you want. Always remember, clear goals manifest clear outcomes.

Today, I choose to relax
knowing that everything is
working out for my highest
good.

WHAT YOU FOCUS ON
MULTIPLIES
if we want to achieve great
things, we must be intentional
to focus on the right things,
even when chaos arises

A quitter never wins and a winner never quits.

Stay on your hustle and have patience. Focus on long-term success not a short-term ego trip.

The goal is to grow strong on
the inside that nothing on the
outside can affect your inner
wellness without your
conscious permission.

Use your energy to imagine all
the things that can go right.
Instead of feeding it to fear and
what can go wrong, make the
choice on how you invest
your mental energy.
You have the choice to
imagine the best case scenario
for your life.

A secret to happiness is letting every situation be what it is instead of what you think it should be and making the best out of it.

You are
absolutely
capable of creating
the life you can't stop
thinking about. Stop
living in your head.
It's time to make your
dreams happen.

who would you be if you
weren't afraid ?

I ATTRACT
ENERGIES AND SITUATIONS
THAT FILL ME WITH
JOY EVERYDAY.

current vibe:
working for the
lifestyle I
promised
myself.

Day 68

Don't forget you can:

- start late
- be unsure
- start over
- try and fail

And still SUCCEED.

6 months of focus and hard work can put you 5 years ahead of life.

Consistency is more
mportant than perfection.

The pain of self-discipline wil
never be as great as the pain o
regret.

"YOU ARE BUILD
TO HANDLE THE PRESSURE
THAT COMES
WITH YOUR CALLING:"

Focus on the step
in front of you,
not the whole staircase.

One day you will tell your
story of how you overcame
what you went through and it
will be someone else's
inspiration to make it.

"You can't go back and change
the beginning,
but you can start where you
are and change the ending."

"What good are wings without the courage to fly."

REMEMBER
if you play small, you stay
small.
it's okay to want more, be
more. do more.

A smooth sea never made
a skilled sailor.

That dream was
planted in your heart
for a reason.

the fact that you are
trying is the proof
that you are strong.

be patient with yourself,
nothing in nature blooms all
year.

You inspire people
who pretend to not even see
you.
Trust me

THIS MOMENT HAS PURPOSE
This season in your life has a
meaningful part in your story
The Divine is adding beauty to
your journey and restoring
peace to your soul.

BE
THE
ENERGY
YOU
WANT
TO
ATTRACT

We cannot become
what we want
be remaining what
we are.

keep going, love.
all this hard work
will be so worth it in
the end.

REMEMBER
WHY
YOU
STARTED.

Change your thoughts
and
you will change your world.

Hold the vision,
Trust the process

I am rich in all areas of my life.

A fit body,
a calm mind,
a house full of love.
These are things that
can't be bought – you
must earn them

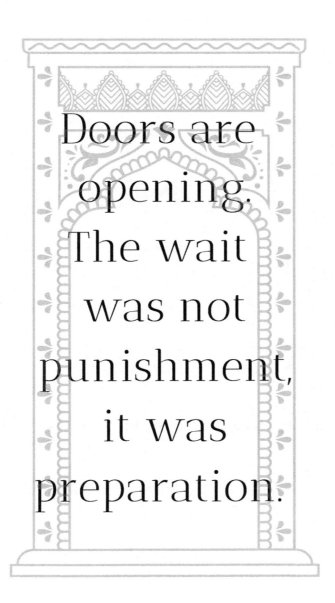

Doors are opening. The wait was not punishment, it was preparation.

You got to start thinking like you're blessed, talking like you're blessed and acting like you're blessed.

That's how you activate your blessings.

I deserve it all.
The family.
The career.
The love.
The peace.
THE LIFE.

The grass is only as green as your mindset. If you're at peace internally, then wherever you stand, will be nourished and fruitful.

You manifest your entire life. Control your thoughts. YOU HAVE POWERS.

Train your mind to see the good in every situation.

YOU ARE THE GREATEST

PROJECT

YOU WILL EVER WORK ON.

A
beautiful day
begins
with a
beautiful mindset

DO IT
FOR YOUR
FUTURE SELF.

THE WORDS YOU SPEAK BECOME THE HOUSE YOU LIVE IN.

Printed in Great Britain
by Amazon

39439256R00059